CW00731874

Eyes in Space

PERSEVERANCE'S EYES

Read With You
Center for Excellence in STEAM Education

Text & illustration copyright © 2022 Read With You
Images courtesy of NASA/ESA/JPL-Caltech.
All rights reserved. No part of this book may be reproduced, stored in a retrieval system, or transmitted in any form or by any means, electronic, mechanical, photocopying, recording, or otherwise, without express written permission of the publisher.
Published by Read With You Publishing
Designed by Read With You Center for Language Research and Development
Read With You and associated logos are trademarks and/or registered trademarks of Read With You L.L.C.
ISBN-13: 979-8-88618-146-3
First Edition April 2022
Printed in the United States of America.

Hi! I'm Perseverance. Just like Curiosity,
I'm a Mars rover packed with instruments.

These are the parts of the spacecraft that flew me to Mars! I'm tucked under the heat shield at the bottom.

When I got close to the planet, the spacecraft part above me dropped me down to the surface.

My main job is to explore the crater Jezero.
It might have once had lakes!

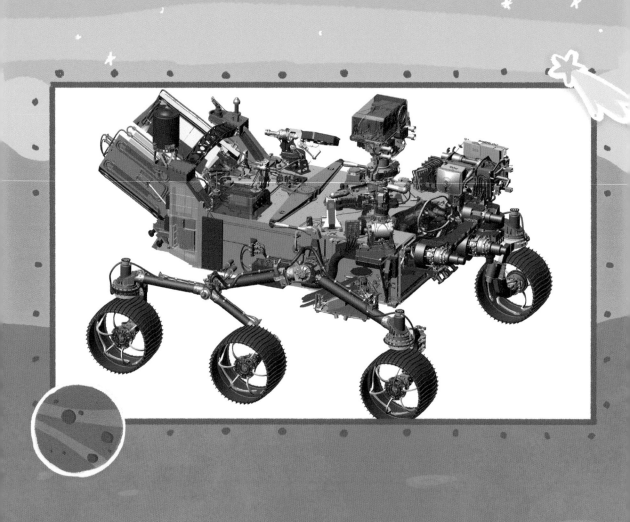

I have a lot to do, so I'm packed with science instruments, lots of cameras, and two microphones.

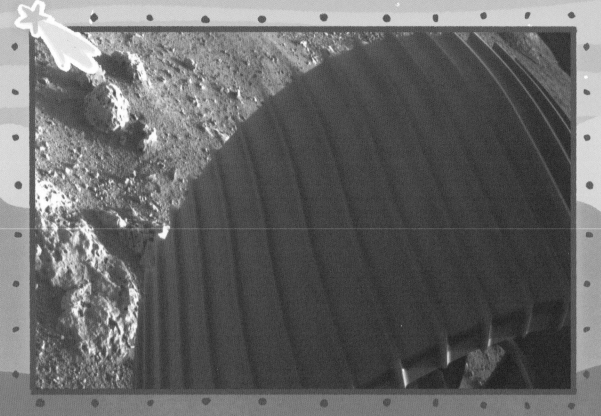

I'm as big as a car.

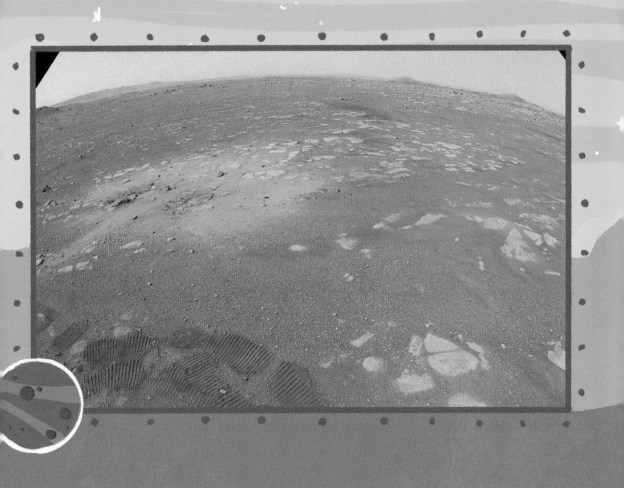

My chunky wheels let me travel over bumpy craters.

I drill into rocks. Then, I make packages of many kinds of Martian dirt and rocks.

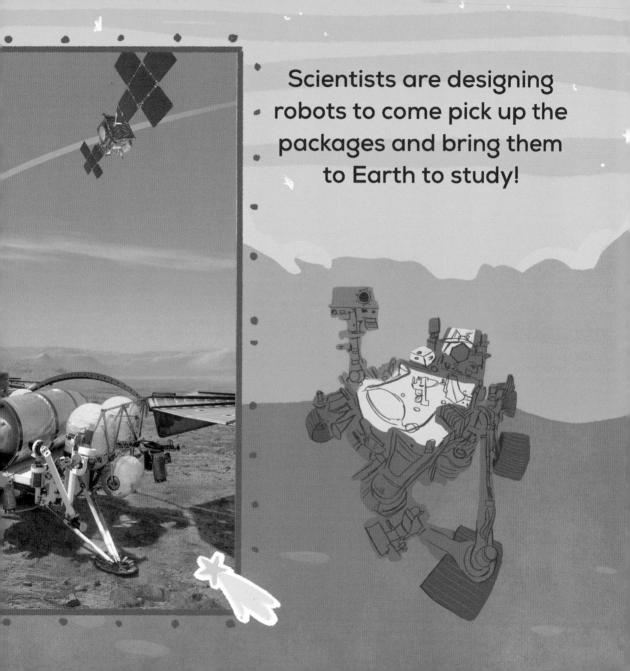

Scientists are designing
robots to come pick up the
packages and bring them
to Earth to study!

I also carry a helicopter. Ingenuity is the first helicopter to fly on a planet other than Earth.

I love getting to explore this wild planet!
Let's see what I find next.

Answer

1. Why is Perseverance exploring Jezero?

2. What do you think Perseverance can hear with its microphones?

3. What is special about Ingenuity?

Answers: 1. It is a crater that might have had lakes once! 2. Answers will vary; encourage thoughtful creativity. 3. It is the first helicopter to fly on another planet.

Learn

Ask an adult to look up more pictures from the Perseverance rover with you. What has it seen? Can you find audio clips from its microphones?

Make

Find a small box. Imagine that you can put five items in it for an alien on another planet to study! What items will you put in? What will those items tell the alien about Earth?

For fun space facts and coloring pages, visit
www.readwithyou.com/collections/eyes-in-space.

Printed in Great Britain
by Amazon

37382470R00016